A VOICE OF MY OWN

The characters in this book communicate in different ways. Can you work out what they mean through their voices, gestures and expressions?

With growing concerns around mental health, and in the wake of a period of uncertainty and change, it is more important than ever to pay attention to how young children express their emotions, and to teach them to articulate their thoughts in a healthy way. This beautifully illustrated picture book has been created to teach children about the importance of communication, both in finding their own 'voice' and listening to others, however they communicate. By demonstrating how easy it can be to interpret a non-verbal communication system, it encourages children to notice and talk about non-verbal cues, giving them the opportunity to actively listen and reassuring them that they will be listened to.

When it comes to child and adolescent mental health issues, prevention and early intervention are key. The 'serve and return' format of this book provides a virtual space where children can explore thoughts and feelings, teaching them that they can feel safe and heard.

Louise Jackson is a teacher, trainer and author who draws on her direct experience of working with children in schools to develop educational materials that are designed to promote participation, relationships and conversation. She has worked on 'closing the gap' projects with national charities, local authorities, schools, children's centres and training organisations to address educational disadvantage, finding new ways to build capacity and resilience across early childhood services and local communities.

Privileged to have worked alongside many inspirational teachers, practitioners and volunteers in educational settings where vulnerable children are thriving, Louise seeks to capture in her research and writing what it is that makes the difference for young children. Working in collaboration with illustrator Katie Waller, she has created a series of books and practical tools which will help local communities, parents, practitioners and teachers understand the valuable role they can all play in cultivating resilience in early childhood.

A practical guide for early years practitioners
and four children's picture books to
use with 4–6-year-olds.

A VOICE OF MY OWN

A Thought Bubbles Picture Book About Communication

Louise Jackson
Illustrated by Katie Waller

Routledge
Taylor & Francis Group

LONDON AND NEW YORK

Cover image credit: Katie Waller

First published 2022
by Routledge
2 Park Square, Milton Park, Abingdon, Oxon OX14 4RN

and by Routledge
605 Third Avenue, New York, NY 10158

Routledge is an imprint of the Taylor & Francis Group, an informa business

© 2022 Louise Jackson and Katie Waller

The right of Louise Jackson to be identified as author of this work and Katie Waller to be identified as illustrator of this work has been asserted by them in accordance with sections 77 and 78 of the Copyright, Designs and Patents Act 1988.

Trademark notice: Product or corporate names may be trademarks or registered trademarks, and are used only for identification and explanation without intent to infringe.

British Library Cataloguing-in-Publication Data
A catalogue record for this book is available from the British Library

Library of Congress Cataloging-in-Publication Data
Names: Jackson, Louise, 1964- author. | Waller, Katie, illustrator.
Title: A voice of my own : a thought bubbles picture book about
communication / Louise Jackson ; illustrated by Katie Waller.
Description: Milton Park, Abingdon, Oxon ; New York, NY : Routledge, 2022.
Identifiers: LCCN 2021028747 (print) | LCCN 2021028748 (ebook) | ISBN
9781032135885 (paperback) | ISBN 9781003229964 (ebook)
Subjects: LCSH: Interpersonal communication in children--Juvenile
literature. | Body language in children--Juvenile literature.
Classification: LCC BF723.C57 J33 2022 (print) | LCC BF723.C57 (ebook) |
DDC 155.4/136--dc23/eng/20211004
LC record available at https://lccn.loc.gov/2021028747
LC ebook record available at https://lccn.loc.gov/2021028748

ISBN: 978-1-032-13588-5 (pbk)
ISBN: 978-1-003-22999-5 (ebk)

DOI: 10.4324/9781003229995

Typeset in Madeleina Sans
by Deanta Global Publishing Services, Chennai, India

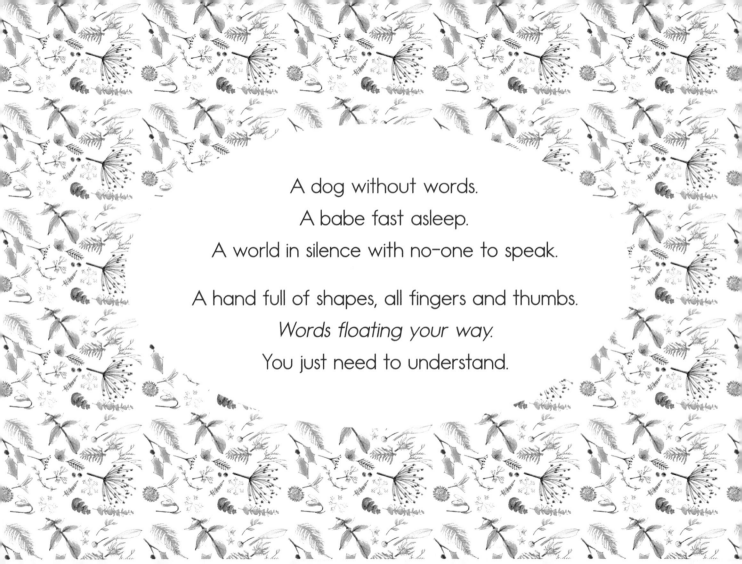

A dog without words.

A babe fast asleep.

A world in silence with no-one to speak.

A hand full of shapes, all fingers and thumbs.

Words floating your way.

You just need to understand.

Follow the pictures.
Take note of the signs.

Search for the meaning.
Read between the lines.

Barking, whining and gnashing of teeth.
Jumping, licking, yapping at your feet.

Can this dog talk?

What do you think?

This little dog needs *you* to make the link.

A tiny baby, all lost and alone.

No-one to listen, she wants to go home.

Stop, look and listen and then you'll see
where this cool baby really wants to be.

SALUT!

CIAO!

سلام, چطوری؟

A jumble of speech, so many voices, words and scripts.
What does he say? Can you hear? What's up?

你好

HALLO!

Привéтик!

Stay a while, watch and wait ...
Try to understand, it's not too late.

A hand full of fingers, moving this way and that.
Hands up, hands down, turn around, hold on to your hat!

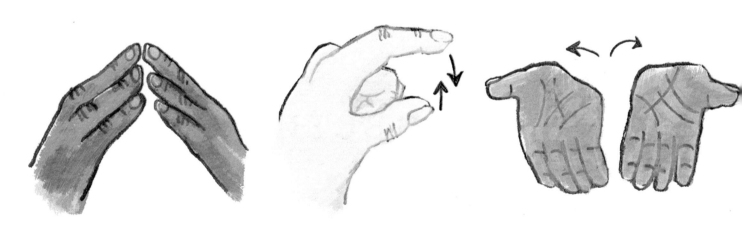

Try using your hands to make gestures and signs.
Let your fingers do the talking without a sound.

So now it's your turn to speak.
Without words what can you say?

Just watch, wait and listen.
Can your friends find a way?

What did you do?
What difference did you make?
Whose voice did you hear?

What change
can you make?

A dog without words.

A babe fast asleep.

A world in silence with no-one to speak.

A hand full of shapes, all fingers and thumbs.

Words floating your way.

Someone to understand.

You followed the pictures,
took note of the signs,

searched for the meaning,
read between the lines.